ANIMAL HEROES

ANIMAL HEROES

THE WOLVES, CAMELS,
ELEPHANTS, DOGS, CATS,
HORSES, PENGUINS,
DOLPHINS, AND OTHER
REMARKABLE ANIMALS
THAT PROVED THEY
ARE MAN'S BEST FRIEND

By Julia Moberg

ILLUSTRATIONS BY JEFF ALBRECHT STUDIOS

MoonDance

Quarto is the authority on a wide range of topics.
Quarto educates, entertains, and enriches the lives of our readers—
enthusiasts and lovers of hands-on living.
www.quartoknows.com

For Mom and Dad, my heroes. —JM

MoonDance

6 Orchard Road, Suite 100
Lake Forest, CA 92630
quartoknows.com
Visit our blogs at quartoknows.com

Printed in China
1 3 5 7 9 10 8 6 4 2

I'm sure you've heard of Spiderman,
Thor, and Batman too.
You know Wonder Woman, the Hulk,
And all the X-Men crew.
Through comics, toys, and movies
They continually amaze,
But there are real-life heroes
Who also deserve praise.
A potbelly pig named LuLu
Came to her owner's aid.
A police dog known as Bum
Chased down renegades.
Wojtek, a brown bear,
Served in World War II.
Jambo, a gorilla,
Made a notable rescue.
A choking girl was saved
By a parrot named Willie.
A dolphin called Filippo
Freed a teen boy from the sea.
Yes, these animals are heroes
And their stories should be told.
So turn the page for more
Tales and histories to behold . . .

Contents

Clever Cats

In ancient Egypt,
Hard times had fallen.
For the country, it seems,
Had a rat problem.
Rats poisoned the food,
And people got sick.
A solution was needed,
And needed real quick!
Then, came along
Wild street cats,
Who, as it turned out,
Loved to eat rats.
And, as a thank-you
For saving their hides,
The people let
The cats come inside.

DID YOU KNOW?

➤ Cats were domesticated in Egypt sometime around 2000 BCE.

➤ In addition to rats, cats also protected people from mice and snakes.

➤ The ancient Egyptians held cats in very high regard. Many gods and goddesses in the ancient Egyptian religion were associated with cats, including Bastet, the goddess of cats.

➤ In ancient Egypt, harming or killing a cat—even accidentally—was considered a severe crime, often punishable by death.

➤ When a cat died, its body was mummified and buried in a tomb. The cat's human family would go into mourning, and members would shave their eyebrows off as a sign of their loss.

TELL ME MORE!

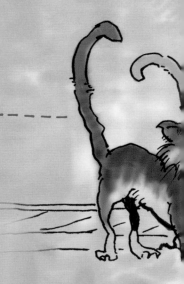

▷ It is not known exactly when cats were first domesticated worldwide. Archaeologists believe it was somewhere between 9,500 and 12,000 years ago.

▷ Cats are the most popular pet in the United States.

▷ Cats spend between 30 and 50 percent of the day grooming themselves. Self-grooming cleans them off, improves circulation, and provides comfort.

▷ Cats can drink seawater. Unlike humans, a cat's kidneys can filter salt out of water.

▷ Because of a genetic mutation, cats are unable to taste sugar.

▷ Male cats tend to be left-pawed, while female cats are usually right-pawed.

The Stouthearted She-Wolf

Twin boys were born,
According to lore,
Then put in a basket,
And sent offshore.
On the Tiber River
They wailed and they cried,
Till a nearby she-wolf
Found them outside.
She cared for the boys,
Her own little brood.
She warded off danger
And supplied them with food.
Little did she know
That when they were grown,
They would then build
The city of Rome.

DID YOU KNOW?

- According to Roman mythology, Romulus and Remus were born in 771 BCE. They were the sons of a princess named Rhea Silvia and Mars, the god of war.
- The king of the city where the boys lived was scared that the twins would overthrow him and take his throne, so he put the boys in a basket on the Tiber River.
- The she-wolf who found the boys cared for and protected them from other animals. Eventually a shepherd found the boys and took them home.

TELL ME MORE!

- One day, after the twins had grown up, Remus was captured and taken to the nearby king. Romulus gathered some shepherds and rescued his brother. When the citizens learned who they were, they offered the boys joint crowns to rule their city.
- The boys turned down the crowns because they wanted to create their own city. They set out to find the perfect spot to build it.
- They decided to build a city in the spot where Rome is located today; however they each wanted to place the city on a different hill. They decided to wait for a sign from the gods. Remus saw a sign of six vultures, but Romulus saw twelve.
- Romulus began building his wall around Palatine Hill. Remus became jealous and made fun of his brother's wall. In retaliation, Romulus killed Remus.
- Romulus officially founded the city of Rome on April 21, 753 BCE, making himself king and naming the city after himself.

Courageous Camels

In December of five forty-seven BCE,
In the city of Thymbra, found in modern Turkey,
A battle was fought between two heads of state:
Croesus from Lydia and Cyrus the Great.
The Lydian army was six times the size,
But Cyrus's army had quite a surprise.
Alongside his soldiers, who marched into war,
Towering above them was a great camel corps.
Three hundred camels were used to attack
The Lydian army, who began to run back.
In the end, Cyrus conquered their land
Thanks, in part, to his camel command.

DID YOU KNOW?

➤ Cyrus the Great used the camel corps alongside his best soldiers to attack the Lydian army from the sides. This caused the Lydian horses and soldiers to turn and run in fear.

➤ Historians believe Cyrus's camels were the first recorded use of camels during war. After his victory, camels were used in battles all over Asia and the Middle East.

➤ Cyrus the Great was the founder and king of the First Persian Empire. He built his empire by conquering and liberating the Median Empire, the Lydian Empire, and the Neo-Babylonian Empire.

➤ Cyrus respected the different religions and customs of the lands he conquered. As a ruler, he was praised for his fair politics and achievements in human rights.

➤ After his death, Cyrus's dynasty remained strong and lasted over two hundred years, until Alexander the Great conquered the empire in 331 BCE.

TELL ME MORE!

▷ There are two types of camels. Dromedary camels have only one hump and live in North Africa, the Middle East, Australia, and western Asia. Bactrian camels have two humps and are found in central and eastern Asia.

▷ Camels have three eyelids and two rows of eyelashes. The third eyelid opens and closes from side to side and cleans off their eyes. It is also thin enough to see through, allowing camels to shield their eyes from the sand, but still see where they are going.

▷ Camels store fat in their humps. They can live off this fat when no food or water is available.

Daring Delta

When a volcano erupted
In the city of Pompeii,
Eighteen hundred years later
A discovery was made.
A dog had been found,
Her collar intact,
And on it there were
Three interesting facts.
Turns out the dog
Had saved her master,
Three times, in fact,
From several disasters.
The first time she pulled
Him out of the sea.
The second, fought thieves
Until he was free.
The third time she fought
A wolf that attacked
And chased it away
Down a dirt track.
Yes, Delta, the dog,
Really saved the day,
Which is why she is called
The Hero of Pompeii.

DID YOU KNOW?

➼ Pompeii was an ancient Roman city near modern-day Naples. It was destroyed and buried underground after the volcano Mount Vesuvius erupted in 79 CE.

➼ In the late 1700s, archaeologists discovered that the bodies of the victims had decomposed and formed casts in the lava sediment.

➼ The cast of Delta's body was found lying over the body of a young child. It is believed that the dog tried to save the child's life after the volcano erupted.

➼ The child that Delta tried to save may have been a sibling of the dog's owner, Severinus.

TELL ME MORE!

▷ Pompeii was a typical Roman city. There was a giant forum, several temples, and even a large amphitheater for gladiator games. An aqueduct carried into the city water that was used in the fountains and public baths.

▷ When Mount Vesuvius erupted, historians estimate that 1.5 million tons of ash and rock shot out of the volcano every second. Some people managed to escape, but most didn't. It is estimated that 16,000 people perished.

▷ Today Pompeii is a popular tourist destination. Approximately 2.6 million people visit the site every year.

Steadfast Steeds

In the thirteenth century,
Genghis Khan reigned
Over the Mongol Empire
And seized quite a domain.
Deep into China,
His army advanced
And the Persian Empire
Had no chance.
Khan's greatest weapon
Had four legs, not two.
They were fast as could be,
Into battle they flew.
On horseback, his men
Would charge at their foe,
And take them all down
With arrow and bow.
Because of his steeds,
He was a fighting machine
And the greatest conqueror
The world's ever seen.

DID YOU KNOW?

➤ Genghis Khan was the first person to take advantage of a horse's strength during combat. The horses played an integral part in his military tactics.

➤ Each soldier owned three to four horses and would rotate riding on each so that no horse would have to bear the rider's weight for long periods of time.

➤ Before combat, each horse's body was covered with armor. A leather covering was placed over the horse's head for protection.

➤ Female horses (mares) were preferred because they provided the soldiers with milk that the men drank during their travels.

TELL ME MORE!

▶ Genghis Khan grew up in northern Mongolia. His boyhood name was Temujin, and from a young age he rode horses and enjoyed hunting with his brothers.

▶ When he was a teenager, Temujin's father was poisoned by an enemy tribe. Temujin gradually built up his own tribe, and conquered the tribe that had killed his father.

▶ He began conquering other Mongol tribes, and uniting them to create a bigger army. He was given the name Genghis Khan, which means "ruler of all."

▶ From 1210 to 1215, Genghis Khan conquered the Xia and Jin dynasties in China.

▶ He suppressed the Persian Empire of Khwarezmia from 1219 to 1221.

▶ Genghis Khan died in 1227. Some historians believe he died when he fell off his horse.

Cherished Chetak

In the year fifteen hundred
And seventy-six,
In an Indian town
There was growing conflict.
Two emperors, it seems,
Had gone to war
And one of them, Pratap,
Had a horse he adored.
The horse was named Chetak;
Into battle he'd ride,
And rumor has it
He had a blue hide.
When the enemy leader
Charged at them one day
Atop an elephant,
Chetak didn't back away.
Instead, the horse
Galloped right toward
The elephant foe,
And protected his lord.
He fought the elephant,
And took Pratap away,
But sadly did not
Live to see a new day.

DID YOU KNOW?

➤ After carrying Pratap away from danger, Chetak collapsed and eventually died.

➤ Chetak died in the Battle of Haldighati, which was fought on either June 18 or June 21, 1576, between Pratap's Mewar Empire and the Mughal Empire.

➤ Pratap, whose full name was Maharana Pratap, was often called the Rider of the Blue Horse because Indian folklore says Chetak's coat was tinted blue.

➤ After Chetak's death, Pratap built a monument where Chetak fell. It still exists.

➤ The Indian government commissioned a bronze statue of Maharana Pratap riding Chetak. It was erected on a mountain in the city of Udaipur and was dedicated in 2009.

TELL ME MORE!

▷ Maharana Pratap was the leader of an area in northwestern India called Mewar.

▷ Pratap battled the Mughal Empire until his death in 1597. He is often referred to as India's first freedom fighter.

▷ To this day, the towns in the surrounding area throw a big festival each year on Maharana Pratap's birthday.

Diplomatic Dog

After the battle of Germantown,
George Washington found
An unnamed dog
On the battleground.
The dog had a collar;
It belonged to their foe,
And his soldiers did not
Want to let the dog go.
But Washington felt
The little loner
Deserved to return
To his British owner.
So to General Howe
The dog was sent back,
And at the next battle
Howe began to cut back.
The general was touched
And showed mercy to those
Who returned his dog,
Or so the story goes.

DID YOU KNOW?

➤ The battle of Germantown was fought on October 4, 1777, in Germantown, Pennsylvania.

➤ After finding the dog, the American soldiers wanted to keep it as a war prize. General Washington disagreed, saying that the dog was not their enemy.

➤ The note that was returned with the dog was written by Washington's chief staff aide, Alexander Hamilton, and read: "General Washington's compliments to General Howe, does himself the pleasure to return [to] him a Dog, which accidentally fell into his hands, and by the inscription on the Collar appears to belong to General Howe."

➤ General William Howe was grateful, calling the return of his dog an "honorable act." Some historians believe Howe eased up on the colonists after getting his dog back.

TELL ME MORE!

▷ During the American Revolution, George Washington was the Commander-in-Chief of the Continental Army.

▷ The Continental Army consisted of the thirteen colonies that declared their independence from Great Britain: Pennsylvania, New York, New Jersey, New Hampshire, Georgia, Connecticut, North Carolina, South Carolina, Maryland, Delaware, Massachusetts, Virginia, and Rhode Island.

▷ The American Revolution lasted from 1775 to 1781. The colonies won the war, and the United States of America became independent from Great Britain.

▷ George Washington was elected the first president of the United States in 1789, and served for two terms.

▷ George Washington was an avid dog lover and owned many dogs himself.

Trustworthy Tortoise

In eighteen fifty-four,
On a Portuguese privateer,
A tortoise was discovered
By the captain that same year.
The navy kept the creature
And named him Timothy,
And he became the mascot
For many ships at sea.
Aboard the HMS *Queen*,
He served in the Crimean War.
And on the *Princess Charlotte*,
He sailed 'round Singapore.
After serving many years,
Aboard many different ships,
Timothy went to live
In the land of fish and chips.
In England, at a castle,
He roamed the lands, carefree.
But then it was discovered
That Timothy was a she!

DID YOU KNOW?

➤ After Timothy's naval service, the tortoise went to live at Powderham Castle in the late nineteenth century. He lived in the estate's Rose Garden.

➤ In 1926, it was discovered that Timothy was a female tortoise.

➤ Timothy showed a natural instinct for survival. During World War II, Timothy felt the vibrations from nearby bombings, and began to dig her own bomb shelter.

➤ Timothy died in 2004. She was believed to be around 165 years old, and was Britain's oldest resident.

TELL ME MORE!

▷ The Crimean War was fought from October 1853 to February 1856 between the Russian Empire and an alliance of France, the United Kingdom, Sardinia, and the Ottoman Empire. The Russian Empire lost the war.

▷ The Crimean War was the first time journalists and photographers were able to document a war. The electric telegraph allowed news to travel across continents within a few hours.

▷ A group of tortoises is called a *creep*.

▷ When they feel threatened, tortoises draw their heads and all their limbs into their shells for protection.

Audacious Abe

In the Civil War,
An eagle named Abe
Was the official mascot
Of a Union brigade.
She often was seen
At parades and events,
And lived with the soldiers
In her very own tent.
During combat,
She'd fly overhead
And screech at the enemy
Until they all fled.
Photos of Abe
Were sold near and far,
And the money helped soldiers
Hurt in the war.
Yes, Abe was a hero
And went on to become
Much more than a mascot:
A sign of freedom.

DID YOU KNOW?

➤➤ Old Abe was the mascot for the Eighth Regiment Wisconsin Volunteers (the Eagle Regiment) of the Union Army. She was named after President Abraham Lincoln and served in more than thirty battles.

➤➤ Under orders from their officers, Confederate troops made several attempts to capture the eagle, but they never succeeded.

➤➤ When she retired, Old Abe went to live in the Wisconsin state capitol building. She had her own two-room apartment, a bathtub, and her own caretaker.

➤➤ She became a nationally known celebrity and appeared at events all around the country.

➤➤ In February 1881, a fire broke out at the Wisconsin capitol building. Old Abe raised an alarm, and it was put out quickly. However, she had inhaled a large amount of smoke and a month later she passed away in the arms of her caretaker.

➤➤ A replica of Old Abe is on display at the Wisconsin state capitol.

TELL ME MORE!

▷ The American Civil War was fought between the southern and northern states of the United States from April 12, 1861, to May 9, 1865. The northern states won.

▷ When the southern states broke away from the country, they named themselves the Confederate States of America. The eleven states that made up the Confederacy were Alabama, Arkansas, Florida, Georgia, Louisiana, Mississippi, North Carolina, South Carolina, Tennessee, Texas, and Virginia.

▷ The northern states, called the Union, were California, Connecticut, Delaware, Illinois, Indiana, Iowa, Kentucky, Maine, Maryland, Massachusetts, Michigan, Minnesota, Missouri, New Hampshire, New Jersey, New York, Ohio, Oregon, Pennsylvania, Rhode Island, Vermont, and Wisconsin. Kansas, Nevada, and West Virginia joined the Union during the war.

Brave Bum

In the early nineteen-hundreds,
In Little Italy,
A mangy mutt named Bum
Showed his bravery.
He served as a police dog
In the notorious Five Points,
Saved many lives from fires,
And other gangster joints.
With New York's Twelfth Precinct,
He'd roam the streets at night,
Responding to a call
Or breaking up a fight.
And from a humane group
That helped animals in need,
Bum received a medal
For his heroic deeds.

DID YOU KNOW?

➤➤ In July 1908, a yellow dog named Bum was rescued by Patrolman Cornelius O'Neil, and became the mascot of the Twelfth Precinct of the New York City Police Department.

➤➤ Bum served the police department for more than eight years, saving countless lives.

➤➤ When responding to a fire, Bum would lead the police and firefighters through smoke-filled tenement buildings to windowless rooms, where people were often huddled together with no way to get out.

➤➤ In July 1912, Bide-a-Wee Home, a nonprofit organization, presented Bum with a bronze medal that was inscribed "Bum, Twelfth Precinct" on one side.

TELL ME MORE!

▷ During the early 1900s, the Little Italy neighborhood of New York City was home to poor immigrants who lived in tenement buildings.

▷ Tenement buildings were often very crowded, dirty, and disease-ridden. They easily caught fire because of poor air circulation.

▷ The Italian Mafia, an organized group of criminals, operated out of Little Italy in the early 1900s. It ran pool halls, bars, and illegal gambling spots.

▷ Because of the Italian Mafia and the poor living conditions, violence was common in Little Italy and the surrounding "Five Points" neighborhoods.

Resolute Rigel

Rigel, a Newfoundland,
Went to sea one day,
Aboard the famed *Titanic*,
Toward New York Bay.
But when it struck an iceberg,
The boat began to sink
And his owner, William Murdoch,
Was gone within a blink.
As many people scrambled
Onto all of the lifeboats,
Rigel swam among them,
And tried to stay afloat.
When another ship approached,
The people tried to call,
But their voices didn't carry
Among the icy squall.
Then Rigel, cold and tired,
Began to bark real loud,
Till finally the boat heard
And rescued the poor crowd.

DID YOU KNOW?

- The rescue boat *Carpathia* saved 705 people from drowning.
- The *New York Herald* wrote about Rigel's heroic efforts in saving some of the *Titanic* passengers.
- Rigel was adopted by one of the *Carpathia*'s crewmen, who retired and took the dog with him to live in Scotland.
- Despite newspaper stories and eyewitness accounts, some historians question the validity of the story because they don't believe William Murdoch had a dog on the ship.

TELL ME MORE!

- The *Titanic* was 882 feet in length and 175 feet tall. In its time, it was considered the largest and most luxurious ocean liner ever built.
- The *Titanic* left Southampton, England, on April 10, 1912. It stopped in France and Ireland before departing for New York.
- On the evening of April 14, 1912, the ship hit an iceberg and began to sink. The iceberg was about 100 feet tall.
- Even though there were enough lifeboats for around 1,200 people, only 705 people survived and 1,503 people died.
- Despite their large size, Newfoundland dogs are good swimmers. They were originally used by fishermen to pull in their nets, carry boat lines to shore, and rescue people.

Peaceful Penguins

In the year nineteen thirteen,
In majestic Scotland,
The Edinburgh Zoo
Received some new friends.
A flock of king penguins
For the zoo were bestowed,
By the country of Norway
For the new zoo abode.
They stood for goodwill
Between the two nations
And they're still there today—
Well—the next generation.
In fact, one in particular,
Who is named Nils Olav,
Was recently knighted
At a service one fall.
The two countries have always
Had good relations,
Perhaps due in part
To this penguin population.

DID YOU KNOW?

➤ When it opened in 1913, the Edinburgh Zoo was the first to house and breed penguins in captivity.

➤ When the Norwegian King's Guard Army visited the zoo sixty years later, it adopted a penguin and named him Nils Olav, after the king of Norway at the time, King Olav V.

➤ When Nils Olav passed away in 1987, his son, Nils Olav II, took over his position.

➤ Nils Olav was knighted on August 15, 2008, in a lavish ceremony. Hundreds of people, including 130 guardsmen watched as the penguin received his knighthood.

➤ Bronze statues of Nils Olav can be found at both the Edinburgh Zoo and the Royal Norwegian Guard base in Oslo, Norway.

TELL ME MORE!

◗ King penguins are native to sub-Antarctic islands.

◗ They have orange spots on their necks and around their ears.

◗ They eat small fish, squid, and crustaceans.

◗ When hunting for food, they swim to depths of 350–1,000 feet and can spend upwards of five minutes underwater without having to come up for air.

◗ On land, king penguins walk slowly from side to side and slide across the ice on their bellies.

Bighearted Baboon

Jackie, a baboon,
Served in World War I
For an African brigade
And was beloved by everyone.
From Egypt on to France,
He marched beside the troops,
Entertained the men,
And at night, watch o'er the group.
In Belgium and in France,
He fought in the front lines,
Lived in muddy trenches,
And watched for deadly mines.
When his men were hurt,
Next to their beds he'd stay,
Lick their wounds all night,
And help them through the day.
After shrapnel hit his leg,
In rural Germany,
He was quickly rushed
Into surgery.
So, he then retired
And his service came to an end,
And the men in his brigade
Sure missed their furry friend.

DID YOU KNOW?

➤ Jackie was enlisted into the South African Army on August 25, 1915. He was the mascot of the Fourth Regiment of the First South African Infantry brigade.

➤ Because he could hear and smell better than humans could, Jackie often detected the enemy's presence.

➤ After being injured in 1918, Jackie was awarded a medal of honor and was promoted to corporal.

➤ After the war, Jackie helped the Red Cross raise money for wounded soldiers by appearing at fund-raisers and taking part in parades.

➤ Baboons use about thirty sounds to communicate with one another. They also use signs to communicate as well, such as shrugging their shoulders or smacking their lips.

➤ Unlike monkeys, baboons cannot grip tree branches with their tails. As a result, they are terrestrial animals, meaning they spend most of their time on the ground.

TELL ME MORE!

▷ World War I began on July 28, 1914, and ended on November 11, 1918.

▷ There were two alliances fighting each other in World War I. The first was the Allied Powers, which included France, England, Japan, Russia, the United States, and Belgium. The second was the Central Powers, which included Germany, Austria-Hungary, the Ottoman Empire, and Bulgaria. The Allied forces won the war.

▷ Baboons live in troops that consist of about fifty baboons total. This typically includes fifteen females and their children, and around eight mature males.

Sergeant Stubby

In World War I,
In western France,
A stray Boston terrier
Was given a chance
To enlist into
The army corps,
And for seventeen battles
He served in the war.
He lived with the men
In the trenches of France,
And once caught a German
By the seat of his pants.
He saved his battalion
From a mustard gas attack,
And for comforting the wounded
He had a special knack.
He received many medals
And became a celebrity.
Yes, this is the story
Of Sergeant Stubby!

DID YOU KNOW?

➤ In July 1917, Stubby was adopted by soldiers training in New Haven, Connecticut.

➤ One of the soldiers smuggled Stubby aboard the troop's ship to France. When he was discovered on board, Stubby saluted the commanding officer. The officer was so amazed he agreed that Stubby could stay.

➤ In April 1918, his leg was wounded by a German hand grenade. He recovered and returned to the trenches.

➤ Stubby could detect incoming gunfire before the soldiers could and would warn his unit to find shelter.

➤ After helping to free a French town from German forces, some of the townswomen presented Stubby with a handmade coat decorated with medals.

➤ After returning to the US, Sergeant Stubby received many medals and awards for his service. He met Presidents Woodrow Wilson, Calvin Coolidge, and Warren G. Harding.

TELL ME MORE!

▷ Boston terriers were first bred in Massachusetts, where they are also the official state dog.

▷ Boston terriers have black and white tuxedo-like coloring and are often nicknamed "American Gentlemen."

▷ Typically, Boston terriers are easy to train and make great guard dogs.

Trusty Tang

A ship hit some rocks
Near a Canadian coast,
And it seemed like everyone
On board would be toast.
The crew tried to throw
Their ropes toward the beach,
But time after time,
The ropes wouldn't reach.
Then Tang, a Newfoundland
Who was also on board,
Jumped in the water
And swam toward the shore.
With a rope in his mouth,
He pulled as he swam,
And he didn't stop
Till he reached the mainland.
Then the people on board
Were pulled one by one,
And each of them lived
'Cause of what Tang had done.

DID YOU KNOW?

➤ Tang saved the lives of all ninety-two people aboard the *Ethie* ship. The youngest passenger was an eighteen-month-old baby girl.

➤ Tang was given a collar from an organization in Philadelphia. It was made of silver, had a starry cross, and the word *Hero* was written across it.

➤ In 1920, the poet E. J. Pratt wrote a poem about Tang's heroics.

➤ Some historians question how and if this story happened. Some believe the dog was on board the ship, while others say he belonged to a villager on shore, and there are those who don't even believe he existed at all!

➤ Despite the speculation about whether the story is true, his silver collar still exists.

TELL ME MORE!

▷ The shipwreck occurred on December 10, 1919. The boat left the town of Cow Head, in Canada's Newfoundland province, and was headed toward the town of Rocky Harbour.

▷ The ship's captain, Edward English, knew that some storm clouds were forming nearby but he chose to sail so that he could get the passengers home for Christmas.

▷ The small storm turned into a treacherous blizzard, and the wind began blowing the ship toward the rocky shore.

▷ Running out of coal, Captain English chose the safest part of the coast to head toward. The ship made its way over a sharp-ridged reef and collided into the rocks.

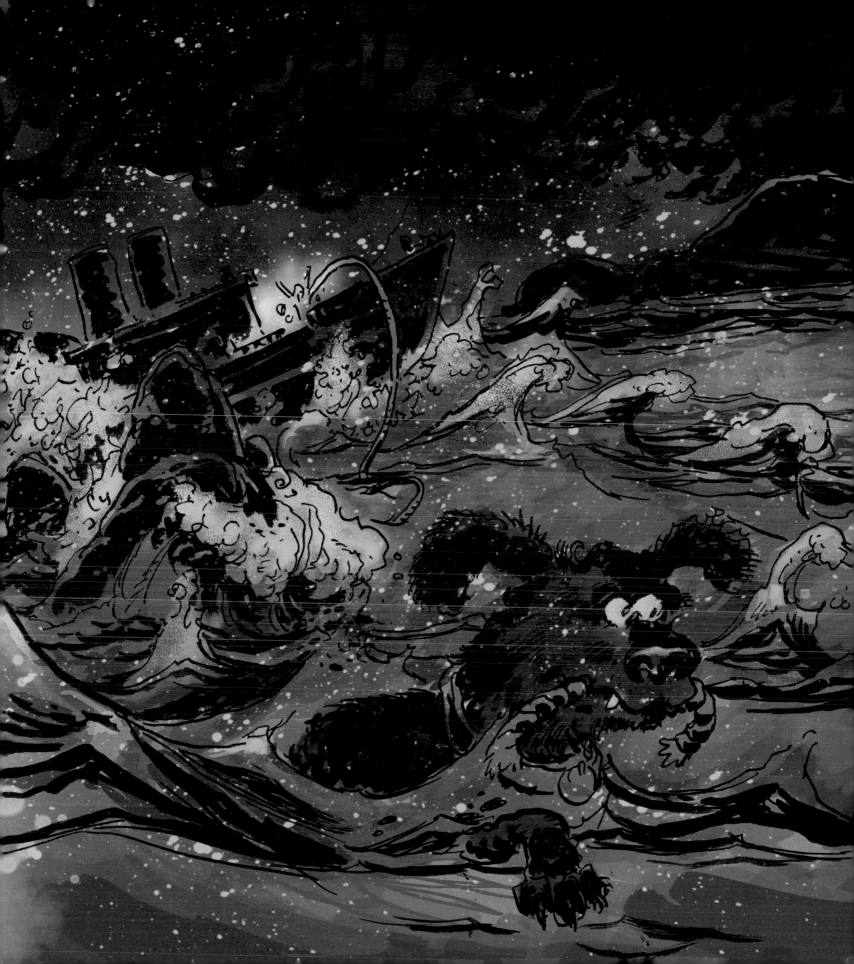

Courageous Commando

As fighting ensued,
During World War II,
To send secret notes,
Pigeons were used.
One, in particular,
Flew more than most.
His name was Commando,
Ninety missions he grossed.
From Germany to France,
He flew like the wind,
While clutching a box
That had memos within.
This info was vital
And helped win the war,
Thanks to Commando
And the brave pigeon corps.

DID YOU KNOW?

➤ For his service, Commando was awarded the Dickin Medal for three important missions he completed in 1942.

➤ In 2015, a plaque commemorating Commando's World War II service was unveiled in Haywards Heath, the town in England where he was born.

➤ During World War II, the British Royal Air Force trained and deployed 250,000 pigeons to fly in the National Pigeon Service.

➤ Most of the pigeons of the National Pigeon Service were parachuted into German-occupied territories, so that the Allied forces there could send back vital information about the German army's whereabouts.

TELL ME MORE!

▷ World War II started when Germany invaded Poland in 1939. France and Great Britain responded by declaring war on Germany.

▷ The war was fought between the Allied Powers (including the United States, Great Britain, and France) and the Axis Powers (including Germany, Japan, and Italy).

▷ Even though the war broke out in Europe, fighting occurred all around the world.

▷ On May 7, 1945, the war in Europe ended when Germany surrendered to Allied forces.

▷ On September 2, 1945, the war in the Pacific Ocean ended when Japan surrendered.

▷ On average, pigeons are able to fly a mile a minute.

Warmhearted Wojtek

In nineteen forty-two,
An unlikely friend
Joined the Polish army
After the capture of Poland.
He wasn't a dog,
Or a cat, or a mare.
No, Wojtek, in fact,
Was a Syrian brown bear.
He lived with the troops
And joined them in war,
Carried boxes of ammo,
And helped even the score.
He captured a thief
In the middle of the night,
Who, as rumor has it,
Ran off in a fright.
After the war,
He retired at a zoo
And his likeness is captured
In many statues.

DID YOU KNOW?

➤ The Polish army came across the bear on April 8, 1942, in Tehran, Persia (modern-day Iran). The army purchased the bear from a young Persian boy.

➤ The soldiers named him Wojtek, which means "joyful warrior."

➤ At first, the soldiers had a hard time feeding him, but they were able to get him to drink condensed milk. He also acquired the taste for marmalade, fruit, honey, and even beer.

➤ Wojtek became a private in the army. He had his own paybook and serial number.

➤ He traveled with the Polish army to Italy, and fought alongside the British army.

➤ At the end of World War II, Wojtek went to Scotland. He became a local celebrity, and an honorary member of the Polish-Scottish Association.

➤ Statues and plaques honoring Wojtek can be found in Poland, Scotland, England, and Canada.

TELL ME MORE!

▷ Syrian brown bears are a subspecies of brown bears. They are native to the Middle East and Caucasia (the region between Europe and Asia).

▷ Because they are rapidly losing their habitat and are hunted by humans, the Syrian brown bear population is quickly declining.

▷ Brown bears have strong shoulder muscles that form a hump on their bodies.

Judicious Jambo

At the Jersey Zoo,
About thirty years ago,
Lived a gentle giant,
A gorilla named Jambo.
A boy fell in his cage one day
And really hurt his head,
And to the young boy's side,
Jambo quickly sped.
He guarded the young lad
And began to stroke his back,
And stopped the other apes
From trying to attack.
Jambo stood his ground
Till an ambulance arrived
And treated the young boy,
Who thankfully survived.
After saving the boy's life,
Jambo's fame increased,
'Cause he also showed the world
That apes are peaceful beasts.

DiD YOU KNOW?

➥ The five-year-old boy fell into the gorilla enclosure on August 30, 1986.

➥ After protecting the boy from harm, Jambo became an international star overnight.

➥ Jambo was the first male silverback gorilla born into captivity.

➥ Jambo passed away on September 16, 1992. In his honor, zoo officials placed a statue of Jambo inside the zoo.

➥ In 2012, Jambo was commemorated on a US postage stamp.

TELL ME MORE!

▷ Gorillas in the wild live in social groups comprised of one adult male, several female gorillas, and their children.

▷ Gorillas groom one another by combing each other with their fingers and teeth. This helps reinforce the group's social bond.

▷ Gorillas are mainly herbivores and eat leaves, shoots, stems, and fruit. They sometimes eat small animals such as caterpillars, snails, and ants.

▷ A gorilla can live for forty to fifty years.

▷ Gorillas have thirty-two teeth.

Generous Ginny

Ginny, a schnauzer
And Siberian breed,
Was also a hero
Who helped those in need.
She had quite a knack
For finding lost cats.
She'd seek them out
In abandoned flats.
In total, she saved
Nine hundred felines
And became the focus
Of several headlines!

➤ After being found in an abandoned building in 1990, Ginny was adopted by a man who suffered from depression. They formed a strong bond, and, in a way, Ginny saved his life too by helping to lift his spirits.

➤ The first time Ginny rescued cats, she found five small kittens trapped in a pipe.

➤ Even though she had a knack for saving cats, Ginny also saved a man's life once. The man, who was blind, was about to walk out into oncoming traffic. She jumped in front of him, and began barking until he turned around, and walked out of harm's way.

➤ In 1998, the Westchester Feline Club named Ginny "Cat of the Year" even though she was a dog.

➤ Ginny passed away on August 25, 2005. She was seventeen years old. More than three hundred cats attended Ginny's memorial service.

TELL ME MORE!

▷ Despite sometimes fighting "like cats and dogs," most times cats and dogs can live peacefully with one another.

▷ Schnauzer dogs were originally bred to hunt small vermin, and as a result they have keen senses of smell and hearing.

▷ Because of their heightened senses, schnauzers make great watchdogs and therapy dogs.

Stalwart Scarlett

In nineteen ninety-six,
In a building in Brooklyn,
Lived a female cat named Scarlett
And her cuddly kitten kin.
When suddenly a fire
Broke out in their abode,
Flames blazed in every corner
Until the fire marshal showed.
To the man's surprise,
Through the fire Scarlett trekked
And carried her kittens,
One by one, each by its neck.
Since Scarlett's eyes were hurt
Within the fire's throes,
To make sure they were safe,
She touched each kitten with her nose.

> ## DID YOU KNOW?

➤ The kittens were only four weeks old when the fire broke out on March 30, 1996.

➤ Because she suffered several bad burns, her eyes were blistered shut by the fire and she couldn't see.

➤ After pulling each cat out, she lined them up together, and gently touched each one with her nose to make sure they were all alive.

➤ The firefighters took Scarlett and her kittens to an animal shelter, where they were given medical treatment.

➤ After the story was featured in newspapers and on television, the shelter received more than seven thousand requests to adopt Scarlett and her kittens.

➤ *National Geographic Kids* magazine included Scarlett on its list of "Ten Cool Cats" from around the world.

➤ Scarlett passed away in 2008 from multiple illnesses.

> ## TELL ME MORE!

▶ Scarlett was a calico cat. A calico cat's fur is mostly white, with black and orange spots.

▶ Due to their genetics, calico cats are almost always female.

▶ Despite popular belief, calico cats are not a distinctive breed. The name refers to their coloration only.

▶ In many cultures, calico cats are believed to bring good luck and fortune to their owners.

▶ In October 2001, the state of Maryland named calico cats as its official state cat.

Lively LuLu

In the state of Pennsylvania,
In nineteen ninety-eight,
A woman named Jo Ann
Almost met her fate.
While vacationing alone,
She had a heart attack,
Which caused her to pass out
And fall onto her back.
Nobody was there
To call or go get help
Except her pet pig LuLu,
Who began to squeal and yelp.
LuLu raced out of the house,
And ran into the street,
Until a car pulled over
And a man jumped from his seat.
LuLu quickly bolted
Into a speedy run,
Then led the man to Jo Ann
And he called 9-1-1.

DID YOU KNOW?

➤ Thanks to LuLu's efforts, help reached Jo Ann in time and she made a full recovery.

➤ If help had arrived fifteen minutes later, doctors believe she wouldn't have survived.

➤ After saving Jo Ann's life, the *New York Times* ran a front-page story about the pig. *USA Today* and *People* magazine also wrote about LuLu.

➤ LuLu appeared on *Live with Regis & Kathie Lee*, the *Late Show with David Letterman*, *Good Morning America*, and *The Oprah Winfrey Show*.

TELL ME MORE!

▶ Because pigs don't have hair, they are very sensitive to the sun. They roll around in mud to stay cool.

▶ Pigs have poor vision, but excellent senses of smell and hearing.

▶ Vietnamese pot-bellied pigs are popular pets because of their small size.

▶ Male pigs are called *boars*, and female pigs are called *sows*.

▶ Pigs have forty-four teeth.

▶ Pigs live on every continent except Antarctica.

▶ Pigs drink up to fourteen gallons of water every day.

Faithful Filippo

Off the coast of Manfredonia,
In southeast Italy,
A fourteen-year-old boy
Fell overboard into the sea.
The boy's name was Davide,
And he didn't know how to swim,
And no one heard him fall,
Or hit the ocean rim.
But underneath the water,
A hero swam nearby.
It was Filippo, a dolphin,
Who heard the teenager's cries.
He pushed him from behind
And kept the boy afloat,
Then swam him back to safety,
Until they reached the boat.

DID YOU KNOW?

➤ In August 2000, Davide fell overboard into the Adriatic Sea. His father was also on board but hadn't heard his son fall in the water.

➤ After Filippo and Davide reached the boat, Davide's father pulled his son back to safety.

➤ Before saving Davide's life, Filippo was well known to fishermen and tourists. After saving Davide's life, he quickly became a local hero and a popular attraction in the area.

TELL ME MORE!

◗ To prevent drowning, wear United States Coast Guard–approved life jackets on boats.

◗ Make sure you know the weather forecast before going out in a boat, and avoid boating when there are strong winds and stormy weather.

◗ Like humans, dolphins are intelligent and very social mammals.

◗ Dolphins live in groups called *pods* or *schools*.

◗ Dolphins communicate with one another by making whistling and clicking noises.

◗ Bottlenose dolphins are the most common dolphins on the planet, and are usually gray.

◗ The smallest known dolphin species is the Maui's dolphin. On average, they weigh ninety pounds and measure four feet long.

Tremendous Trakr

When both towers fell,
That awful, fateful day,
Many answered the call
And rushed there right away.
In addition to the cops,
And the firemen brigade,
A shepherd dog named Trakr
Came to the people's aid.
Trakr searched through the debris,
And among all the rubble,
He detected someone there,
Who was in a lot of trouble.
Under the South Tower,
A woman was found,
Thanks to the efforts
Of one essential hound.

DID YOU KNOW?

➡ Trakr was trained in the Czech Republic and joined the Halifax Regional Police in Canada when he was fourteen months old.

➡ When Trakr's handler, a Canadian police officer, saw the images of the World Trade Center on television, he and Trakr headed to Ground Zero to help the rescue teams.

➡ They arrived on the morning of September 12 and were put to work searching through the debris for any signs of life. The woman Trakr rescued had been stuck in the rubble for twenty-six hours, and was the last person found alive.

➡ Trakr worked at Ground Zero until September 14, when he collapsed from exhaustion and smoke inhalation. He was treated and returned home to Canada.

➡ Trakr passed away in April 2009. Months later, scientists cloned five copies of Trakr using his DNA. The puppies were named Valor, Prodigy, Trustt, Deja Vu, and Solace.

TELL ME MORE!

▷ On September 11, 2001, terrorists hijacked four airplanes and attacked the United States. They flew two of the planes directly into the World Trade Center, two skyscrapers in New York City.

▷ After the planes hit, the buildings caught fire and collapsed.

▷ The terrorists who hijacked the planes were from a terrorist group called Al Qaeda, led by a man named Osama bin Laden.

▷ Following the attacks, the United States sent troops to Afghanistan, a country in the Middle East where Al Qaeda was based.

▷ On May 1, 2011, United States forces found and killed Osama bin Laden in Pakistan.

Hero Horses

Weeks after 9/11,
When America went to war
And invaded Afghanistan,
It was bin Laden they searched for.
A special team of men,
Called the Green Berets,
Stormed the desert plains,
On horseback, all the way.
The horses were all stallions,
And fast as can be,
They advanced on the enemy,
The Taliban, who would flee.
Yes, to the special forces,
These horses were quite vital
In helping win the war
And America's survival.

DID YOU KNOW?

➤ In October 2001, America invaded Afghanistan, the country where Al Qaeda was based. An extreme Islamic group called the Taliban ran the government, and was protecting Al Qaeda's terrorist leader, Osama bin Laden.

➤ The Green Beret special force teams invaded the country on horseback because with the wide-open desert terrain, it was easier for them to travel undetected.

➤ The Afghani tribes who were assisting the Green Berets provided them the horses. Only two of the US soldiers had any experience riding on horseback prior to the invasion.

➤ US-led forces initially brought down the Taliban government in December 2001.

➤ A statue depicting a United States Special Forces soldier riding upon a stallion was erected at One World Trade Center. It was dedicated on November 11, 2011, in a ceremony led by Vice President Joe Biden.

TELL ME MORE!

▷ Horses have been used in war for at least five thousand years. The first recorded use of horses in warfare occurred between 4000 and 3000 BCE in Eurasia.

▷ During World War I, cavalries of horses were being phased out in exchange for tanks and military vehicles.

▷ After September 11, the Department of Homeland Security was formed. Its mission is to protect the United States from terrorism.

Motherly Mandy

In Australia, a farmer
Was out one day,
When suddenly a cow
Came round the way.
He charged at the farmer,
Who was knocked off his feet,
And toppled right over
In the manure heap.
His hip was hurt bad,
He could not move a limb,
He tried calling for help
But nobody heard him.
Then his goat Mandy
Came and laid by his side,
Made him feel safe,
And her milk she supplied.
Throughout the cold nights
She kept him quite warm,
Huddling beside him,
Even during a storm.
For five whole days
She kept him alive,
And in the end,
The farmer survived.

DID YOU KNOW?

- In October 2002, the seventy-eight-year-old farmer was able to survive five days, mainly because he was able to drink the goat's milk for nourishment.
- After five days of being stranded with a broken hip, some friends of his stopped by the farm and found him alive. They called an ambulance, and he received medical attention.
- His collie dog, also named Mandy, stayed by his side as well during the cold nights.

TELL ME MORE!

- Goats are one of the earliest domesticated animals on our planet. It is believed that they were first domesticated around nine thousand years ago.
- A baby goat is called a *kid*. Right after they are born, kids can stand up and walk around.
- Goats like to cuddle. They will curl up next to one another, keeping one another warm.
- Goats communicate by making a noise called a *bleat*. Right after a baby goat's birth, the mother and kid goat can recognize each other's bleats.

Devoted Dory

In England, a man
Suddenly fell asleep.
At least that's what
His wife did think.
Unbeknownst to her,
He had, in fact,
Fallen into a coma
From a diabetes attack.
But Dory, their rabbit,
Came along,
And jumped on his chest,
'Cause something was wrong.
He didn't wake up,
Not a peep, nor a yelp,
And that's how his wife
Knew to call for help.

DID YOU KNOW?

➤ Dory saved the man's life in January 2004.

➤ The man's wife thought he had simply lain down to take a nap after a hard day's work.

➤ After Dory began jumping on the man's chest, his wife realized something was wrong because he wasn't waking up.

➤ His wife called for an ambulance, and paramedics were able to give him some medicine that revived him.

➤ After saving his life, Dory was made a member of the Rabbit Welfare Association.

TELL ME MORE!

▷ Rabbits are highly intelligent animals. They can even be trained to use a litter box.

▷ Because of their long ears, rabbits pick up sounds in every direction. They also use their ears to regulate their body temperature.

▷ Rabbits are herbivores and primarily eat grass, plants, and wildflowers.

▷ Rabbits also eat their own poop! They do this because it contains healthy bacteria that help them absorb nutrients and digest their food.

Reassuring Rojo

In Portland, Oregon,
Rojo, the llama,
Is a therapy animal
Who helps those with trauma.
He comforts the sick,
The downtrodden, and weary.
He reduces their stress,
And his presence is cheery.
From hospitals to schools,
He helps those in need.
Yes, Rojo, the llama,
Is a hero indeed!

➤ Since 2007, Rojo has been a therapy llama at the Mtn Peaks Therapy Llamas and Alpacas center, a nonprofit organization that services Portland, Oregon, and Vancouver, Washington.

➤ Rojo and the other llamas and alpacas at the center go to hospitals, special-needs schools, assisted living communities, and rehabilitation facilities, where they help people dealing with problems and difficult issues.

➤ The llamas and alpacas' presence can reduce stress levels, improve fine motor skills, and help people feel less alone.

➤ Rojo has his own Facebook, Instagram, and Twitter accounts, where he keeps up-to-date with his human friends.

TELL ME MORE!

▶ The first recorded animal therapy practice was in Gheel, Belgium, during the ninth century. Disabled people in the town began to visit with animals on a local farm.

▶ Llamas are native to South America. They were first brought to the United States in the late 1800s and put on display in zoos around the country.

▶ Even though they don't have a hump, llamas are members of the camelid (camel) family.

▶ A baby llama is called a *cria*.

▶ Llamas are often used as guard animals to protect herds of sheep and goats from coyotes and other predators.

▶ Llamas spit when they feel threatened.

Exceptional Elephant

In the Indian Ocean,
In two thousand four,
An earthquake shook
The ocean floor.
It sent a tsunami
Upon the land,
And powerful waves
Hit the coast of Thailand.
Amber, an eight-year-old,
Was out in the sand
Before the waves hit
Down on dry land.
But when the waves came,
Colossal and strong,
Amber was saved
By an elephant, Ningnong.
The elephant swung her
Onto his back,
And ran to high ground
Before the wave thwacked.

DID YOU KNOW?

➤ Amber's family was vacationing in Phuket, Thailand, when the tsunami hit.

➤ Amber had befriended Ningnong, a four-year-old elephant, and spent her days playing with him on the beach.

➤ Before the tsunami hit, Ningnong was acting strange. He kept pulling Amber's arm and trying to run away from the water, as if he sensed something bad was about to happen.

➤ As the killer waves hit the beach, Ningnong swung Amber up on his back, and ran to higher ground. When the water approached them, he turned to the side, shielding her.

➤ As a thank-you for saving Amber's life, her family sends Ningnong's owner 30 British pounds a month (about $40).

TELL ME MORE!

▶ Tsunamis are giant waves of water caused by either volcanic eruptions or earthquakes.

▶ On December 26, 2004, a magnitude 9.1 earthquake struck the ocean floor off the coast of northern Sumatra. This caused a tsunami to hit the coasts of fourteen countries: India, Indonesia, Thailand, Malaysia, the Maldives, Bangladesh, Myanmar, Somalia, Sri Lanka, Kenya, Madagascar, South Africa, Tanzania, and the Seychelles.

▶ The Indian Ocean tsunami was the world's deadliest recorded tsunami. It is estimated that more than 230,000 people lost their lives. Indonesia was hit the hardest, followed by Sri Lanka, India, and Thailand.

▶ The word *tsunami* is a Japanese word that means "harbor wave."

Loyal Lion Pride

On her walk home from school,
Much to everyone's dismay,
An African girl
Was kidnapped one day.
Across Ethiopia,
The cops did what they could,
But the kidnappers were fast,
And it didn't look good.
But suddenly help came
From an unlikely source.
Three lions crossed paths
With the kidnappers' course.
They circled the girl,
Chased the men away,
And stayed by her side
Until help came their way.

DID YOU KNOW?

➤➤ After the lions heard the girl screaming for help, they charged at her kidnappers and chased them away.

➤➤ On June 9, 2005, the police found the girl being protected by the lions. For half a day the lions stayed with her, until they finally backed away.

➤➤ Even though lions typically attack people, wildlife experts believe that they may have thought the girl's cries sounded like a lion cub's meows.

TELL ME MORE!

▷ Ethiopian lions have dark manes and smaller bodies than other lions in Africa do.

▷ Lions live in groups called *prides*, consisting of about fifteen lions. The females do all the hunting, while the male lions defend their land. Despite the females being the hunters, the males always eat first.

▷ Lions sleep up to twenty hours a day.

▷ The US Fish and Wildlife Service estimates that African lions may be extinct by the year 2050. They are protected under the Endangered Species Act.

▷ The greatest threats African lions face are loss of habitat, loss of prey, and encounters with humans.

Kindhearted Katrina

On August twenty-ninth,
In two thousand five,
Along the Gulf Coast,
A hurricane arrived.
It struck the city
Of New Orleans hard.
It damaged the houses
And destroyed many yards.
As the waters rose,
A man started to drown,
But was pulled to safety
By a heroic hound.
Her name was Katrina,
A black Labrador.
She stayed till help came,
And the man was cared for.

DID YOU KNOW?

→→ The dog stayed with the man until a helicopter came to rescue him. Even though the man begged for the dog to go with him, the rescue team said they couldn't take her.

→→ The story was originally featured on a television news show. It was the television staff who went back and rescued the dog. They tried to find her owners, but had no luck. In the end, one of the show's photographers adopted the dog and named her Katrina, after the hurricane.

→→ Katrina was named the guest of honor at the Humane Society of the United States' twentieth annual Genesis Awards.

TELL ME MORE!

▷ Hurricane Katrina was one of the most destructive hurricanes ever to hit America.

▷ It is estimated that more than 1,800 people died, and more than a million people were left without homes.

▷ Hurricane Katrina hit five states: Alabama, Florida, Georgia, Louisiana, and Mississippi.

▷ It cost the United States $108 billion in damages.

▷ Storm waves caused the levees in New Orleans to collapse. Levees are walls built to prevent water from overflowing. Because they collapsed, 80 percent of the city of New Orleans became flooded.

▷ Over ten years have passed since the deadly hurricane hit. Much of New Orleans has recovered, but there are still neighborhoods that haven't been able to rebuild fully.

▷ For the past twenty-five years, the Labrador retriever has held the American Kennel Club's top title as the most popular dog in the United States.

Truehearted Toby

In the city of Calvert,
In the state of Maryland,
A woman was saved
By her faithful doggy friend.
Debbie was eating
An apple one day,
When it suddenly got lodged
In her airway.
She tried beating her chest,
And forcing it up,
But nothing would work,
And then came her pup.
Toby, a two-year-old
Golden retriever,
Jumped onto Debbie,
And did the Heimlich maneuver.

DID YOU KNOW?

➡ On March 23, 2007, Toby noticed Debbie choking. He jumped up on her and pushed her to the ground with his front paws.

➡ Once on the ground, Toby began jumping up and down on her chest, and was able to dislodge the apple from Debbie's windpipe.

➡ Miraculously, Toby's actions are in line with how the American Red Cross and the American Heart Association recommend treating choking victims.

TELL ME MORE!

▷ Dr. Henry Judah Heimlich, an American surgeon, came up with the Heimlich maneuver in 1974.

▷ The Heimlich maneuver is a technique that uses a series of abdominal thrusts to stop someone from choking.

▷ The Heimlich maneuver should only be performed on a person whose airway is completely blocked.

▷ All parents and childcare providers should be trained in techniques that help choking victims. Training is usually available through the American Heart Association, the American Red Cross, and local community centers.

▷ According to the American Kennel Club, golden retrievers are the third most popular dog breed in the US.

Whip-Smart Winnie

One night, a family
Went to sleep in their beds,
But then Winnie, their cat,
Came and nudged at their heads.
She meowed, and she cried,
Tried to get them to wake,
For she sensed danger coming
And knew what was at stake.
Finally, her owner,
Woke up in a haze.
"Something is wrong,"
She thought, in a daze.
Turns out a gas leak
Had occurred in the night,
And Winnie's sixth sense
Sensed something wasn't right.
They called 9-1-1,
And help soon arrived,
And because of their cat,
The whole family survived.

DID YOU KNOW?

➡ The three members of the family were treated for carbon monoxide poisoning on March 24, 2007. They all recovered.

➡ The sheriff's department believed that if they had waited five more minutes to call for help, they probably would not have survived.

➡ This wasn't the first time Winnie saved her family's life. She had previously warned them about nearby tornadoes.

TELL ME MORE!

▷ A cat's sense of smell is about fourteen times stronger than a human's. Cats even have a scent organ in their mouths!

▷ Because they have such heightened senses, cats are able to detect fumes, changes in weather, and even the earth's movements.

▷ Carbon monoxide is an odorless gas that is produced when fuel is burned. If it builds up indoors it can become poisonous to those who breathe it in.

▷ Symptoms of carbon monoxide poisoning include sudden dizziness, headache, upset stomach, vomiting, chest pains, and confusion.

▷ To protect yourself and your family, install a carbon monoxide detector in your home. Make sure to replace the batteries twice a year.

Keen Kerry

In Scotland, a farmer
Was tending her cows,
When suddenly one of the
Cows became roused.
It knocked the woman
Down on the ground,
And prepared to crush
With its six hundred pounds.
Then suddenly, Kerry,
The farmer's trusty steed,
Kicked the cow,
And her owner was freed.
Kerry stayed by her side
Till help came their way,
And got apples and carrots
For saving the day!

DID YOU KNOW?

- In July 2007, the farmer was in the process of taking a mother cow and her calf to a special calf house, when the mother suddenly turned on her.
- The cow knocked her on the ground, and prevented her from getting back up.
- The farmer was moments away from being completely crushed by the cow when her horse Kerry galloped over and intervened.
- After the incident, Kerry would walk alongside anyone who entered the field, protecting the person from any danger.

TELL ME MORE!

- The explorer Christopher Columbus brought the first cattle to the Americas in 1493, when he landed in what is now the Dominican Republic.
- In 1521, the explorer Ponce de León brought Spanish cattle with him to what is now modern-day Florida.
- Just like we have unique fingerprints, the spots on a cow are unique to each individual cow.
- Cows drink enough water every day to fill a bathtub.
- On average, cows sleep four hours a day.

Doughty Dolphins

In two thousand seven,
In Monterey Bay,
A surfer named Todd
Was out surfing waves.
When suddenly a shark
Caught him off guard,
Smacked into his side,
And bit his leg, hard.
But when a school of dolphins
Heard Todd call,
They circled around him,
Creating a wall.
They fought off the shark,
Till he caught the next wave,
And thanks to the dolphins,
Todd's life was saved.

DID YOU KNOW?

➤ The great white shark attacked Todd on August 28, 2007. It was between twelve and fifteen feet long.

➤ After the dolphins performed a protective ring around him, Todd was able to get back on his surfboard and return to shore.

➤ It took him six weeks to recover from his injuries.

➤ Todd still surfs today, even in the same spot where he was attacked.

TELL ME MORE!

▷ Great white sharks search the ocean surface for possible prey. They will bump into their victim first before biting it.

▷ When they're young, great white sharks eat small fish and rays. When they're older they usually feed on seals, sea lions, and small whales.

▷ Scientists believe sharks typically attack and bite humans more so out of curiosity than anything else. We are not their usual prey.

▷ To avoid a shark attack, don't swim in areas that are known to be frequented by sharks. If you are unsure about whether certain areas might contain sharks, ask lifeguards and local authorities before going in the water.

Remarkable Rex

In two thousand eight,
In the land down under,
A dog named Rex
Became quite a wonder.
Walking with his owner,
They came upon
A kangaroo that'd been hit,
And was sadly gone.
They left the 'roo,
And went back home,
But a few hours later,
Rex went back, alone.
In the kangaroo's pouch,
Much to his dismay,
Was a kangaroo baby,
Alive as day.
He carried the joey
All the way up the road,
Until they were safe,
Back at Rex's abode.

DiD YOU KNOW?

➡ The mother kangaroo had been hit by a car in March 2008, and was lying by the side of the road.

➡ After Rex rescued the baby kangaroo (called a *joey*), it began to snuggle with him. Rex, in turn, sniffed and licked the joey.

➡ The baby kangaroo was given the name Rex Jr. in honor of Rex, and was treated at the Jirrahlinga Wildlife Sanctuary in Australia.

➡ When he was fully grown, Rex Jr. was released back into the wild.

➡ Rex is a mix between a German shorthaired pointer and a wirehaired pointer. In general, pointer dogs are good-natured and reliable.

TELL ME MORE!

▶ Kangaroos belong to a class of mammals called *marsupials*. Other marsupials include the koala, wallabies, possums, wombats, and the Tasmanian devil.

▶ Kangaroos hop because they cannot move their legs independently from each other on land. They are able to move them separately underwater.

▶ Kangaroos cannot move backward.

▶ When baby kangaroos are born they are only two centimeters long, about the size of a jellybean!

▶ After they are born, baby kangaroos live in their mother's pouch. Red kangaroos leave the pouch when they are eight months old, while gray kangaroos stay until they are eleven months old.

Chivalrous Chi Chi

On a North Carolina beach,
In two thousand eight,
Two elderly women
Nearly met their fate.
Nobody heard them
Calling from sea,
Except for a Chihuahua,
Whose name was Chi Chi.
He barked loud and clear,
And became very brisk,
Till his owners looked over,
And saw the women at risk.
Chi Chi ran toward the women,
Who continued to shout,
And his owners then quickly
Pulled them both out.

DID YOU KNOW?

➤ One of the women in danger had fallen headfirst into the surf, and the other woman was trying to hold the first woman's head above water. They were both in danger of being carried away by the waves.

➤ After saving the woman's lives in October 2008, Chi Chi was named *Reader's Digest* Hero Pet of the Year.

➤ Chi Chi made his TV debut on the *Today Show*, where he was honored for his heroics.

TELL ME MORE!

▷ Chihuahuas are the smallest dog breed in the world. They are four to nine inches tall, and weigh between four and seven pounds.

▷ Native to Mexico, Chihuahuas were named after the state of Chihuahua in Mexico.

▷ Chihuahuas were originally called the *Arizona dog* or the *Texas dog* because that is where they were first found in the United States.

▷ Chihuahuas live on average for ten to eighteen years, making them one of the longest-living dogs.

▷ Chihuahuas are very loyal dogs. They form close bonds with their owners, and often see themselves as the protector in the relationship.

Wise Willie

In Denver, Colorado,
Willie became
A parrot that received
A whole lot of fame.
After saving the life
Of two-year-old Hannah,
He quickly became
As famous as Santa.
Hannah was eating
While her sitter stepped out,
When suddenly something
Got lodged in her mouth.
Willie, nearby,
Started to shout,
"Mama! Baby! Mama!"
And flapped all about.
The sitter rushed in,
Performed the Heimlich in time,
And thanks to Willie,
Hannah was fine.

DID YOU KNOW?

➡ Willie was a green-feathered Quaker parrot belonging to Hannah's babysitter.

➡ In November 2008, the babysitter was in the bathroom when Hannah started choking.

➡ After saving the little girl's life, Willie was presented with the Animal Lifesaver's Award by the Red Cross.

➡ Both the governor of Colorado and the mayor of Denver attended Willie's award ceremony.

TELL ME MORE!

▶ Quaker parrots are highly intelligent. They can imitate not only words, but also all kinds of sounds including a telephone ringing and a cat's meow.

▶ Choking can occur when a foreign object obstructs someone's airway.

▶ Babies under the age of two are at the highest risk of choking injuries because they have small air passages and immature throat muscles, and they constantly put things in their mouth.

▶ Children under four should avoid common choking foods, such as nuts, hot dogs, popcorn, large pieces of fruits or vegetables, hard candies, gum, and whole grapes.

Manful Mila

In northeast China,
In two thousand nine,
A diving contest
Made worldwide headlines.
A twenty-six-year-old female,
Her name was Yang Yun,
Dove down twenty feet,
And then danger began.
Both of her legs
Suddenly cramped up,
So she tried and she tried
To swim her way up.
When suddenly Mila, a whale,
Came out of the blue,
Pushed her to safety,
And she made it through.

DID YOU KNOW?

➤ The diving contest was held in July 2009 at Polar Land, an aquarium in the city of Harbin, China.

➤ Contestants dove down into the whale pool without any breathing equipment. Whoever stayed down the farthest and longest won the competition.

➤ It was Yang Yun's first time diving that deep, and her legs began to cramp.

➤ Mila used her nose to push Yang Yun back to the water's surface.

➤ After she received medical attention, Yang Yun thanked Mila by diving back into the water.

TELL ME MORE!

▷ Beluga whales have white skin, a round head, and a large forehead.

▷ In the wild, beluga whales inhabit mostly arctic and subarctic waters. They can be found off the coasts of Canada, the United States (Alaska), Norway, Greenland, and Russia.

▷ The word *beluga* comes from the word *bielo* which means "white" in Russian. Their white coloring acts as camouflage among the polar ice caps. It protects them from orca whales and polar bears.

▷ When they are born, beluga whales are dark gray. It takes about seven to eight years for them to develop their white coloring.

▷ Unlike other whales, belugas can nod their heads and even move it in all directions.

▷ Beluga whales can swim backward.

Lionhearted Long Long

In China, a man
Found a sick snake one day,
And he nursed it with herbs
Till it was strong and okay.
He tried to release it
Back into the wild,
But it returned to the man
After a little while.
So he decided to keep it
As a household pet,
And one day it saved him
From a serious threat.
A fire occurred
In the middle of the night,
And with a whip of its tail
The snake urged him to flight.
Some experts argue
If this story is real.
You have to admit,
It's pretty surreal!

DID YOU KNOW?

➤ After adopting the snake, the man named it Long Long.

➤ In the fall of 2009, an electric blanket caught fire in the middle of the night. In order to wake the man up and warn him about the fire, the snake allegedly began to whip him with its tail and grab at his clothes with its teeth.

➤ Reptile experts question the validity of this story, as they believe snakes don't possess the brainpower to warn of this sort of danger.

➤ The man, however, insists the story is true and he believes Long Long saved his life.

TELL ME MORE!

▷ There are more than three thousand different species of snakes on our planet.

▷ Snake scales are made of keratin, the same material from which human fingernails and hair are made.

▷ Snakes shed their skin about three times each year. This process is called *molting*.

▷ Snakes can't close their eyes, and sleep with their eyes open.

▷ One way to tell whether a snake is poisonous or not is to look at its eyes. If it has round pupils, it is nonpoisonous. If it has diamond-shaped pupils, it is poisonous.

Plucky Pinky

Nine-year-old Richie
Was playing outside,
When a swarm of bees
Flew toward his backside.
He ran as fast
As his little legs could,
But the bees stung his ankles
As he ran through the woods.
Suddenly, his dog,
A pit bull named Pinky,
Distracted the bees.
It really was risky.
The bees then went after
Pinky herself,
Who was stung forty times,
And twice in the mouth.
Turns out that Richie
Was allergic to bees,
But he survived the attack
Thanks to Pinky's good deed.

DID YOU KNOW?

➤ On August 29, 2010, Richie was attacked by a swarm of bees. Pinky jumped onto him and the bees began to attack her instead, while Richie ran to safety.

➤ The family rushed Pinky to an animal hospital where it took four to five hours to remove all the bee stings. In the end, she made a full recovery.

➤ Richie suffers from a blood condition. If he had been stung more times than he was, his life would have been at risk.

TELL ME MORE!

▶ Never poke a beehive. The bees inside will do what they can to defend their home.

▶ If bees start attacking you, run as fast as you can until you reach shelter.

▶ Do not try to swat at bees. When a bee is crushed, it emits a smell that attracts more bees.

▶ If you cannot find shelter inside, use blankets, clothes, or anything that can cover you.

▶ Once you've reached shelter, remove any stingers that you can. Scrape them out sideways using your fingernails or the edge of a credit card. Do not pull them out with tweezers, as that will only release more venom into your skin.

▶ If you have been stung more than fifteen times, or if you are allergic to bees, seek medical attention immediately.

Magnificent Masha

In a cold Russian city,
Masha, the cat,
Was trying her hardest
To catch a small rat.
When suddenly she heard
Some cries near the stairs,
She went to explore
And found a box there.
Inside was a baby,
Without enough clothes,
So Masha lay down,
And cuddled him close.
She stayed by his side,
Keeping him warm,
Protecting his body
From a windstorm.
Masha meowed,
Until somebody came,
And then she went on
To receive lots of fame.

DID YOU KNOW?

▸ In January 2015, a baby boy was left in a cardboard box outside of an apartment complex in Obninsk, Russia.

▸ One of the apartment's residents heard the cat meowing, and discovered her curled up with the baby, keeping him warm.

▸ When the baby was rushed to the hospital, Masha tried to follow the paramedics' vehicle.

▸ After the events, Masha was featured in news articles and television programs worldwide.

▸ After hearing about how she saved the baby's life, residents of the building spoiled Masha by giving her extra treats.

TELL ME MORE!

▶ Cats sleep sixteen to eighteen hours every day.

▶ Just like a human's fingerprint, each cat's "nose print" is unique.

▶ Every day in the United States, more than thirty-five thousand kittens are born.

▶ On average, indoor cats live about fifteen years. Outdoor cats usually live only three to five years.

▶ The oldest-known cat was named Puss, who died in 1939 at the age of thirty-six.

▶ Cats have great night vision and only need one-sixth the amount of light that humans need in order to see.

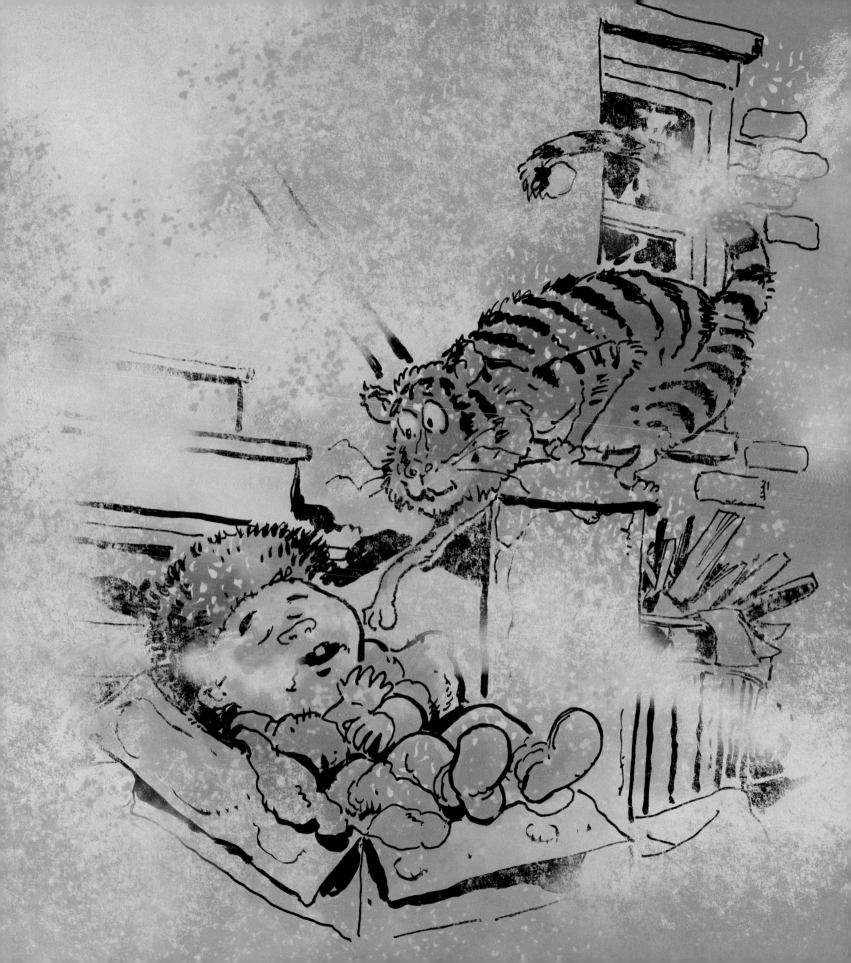

I hope you liked these tales
About such amazing beasts,
Who sacrificed so much
And performed such wondrous feats.
You might also have a pet
Who has proven time again
That its loyalty to you
Is something to commend.
So next time you're at a zoo,
Or look a cat right in the eyes,
Remember heroes come
In different shapes and sizes.

My Animal Hero

Are you proud of your pet? Use this page to celebrate your awesome animal!
Photocopy this page if you have more than one hero or if this book doesn't belong to you!

PLACE YOUR POEM HERE:

_____

_____

_____

_____

_____

_____

DID YOU KNOW?
(pet's age, special talents, breed,
why he or she is a hero to you)

_____

_____

_____

_____

_____

PLACE PHOTO HERE

TELL ME MORE!
(add fun facts about you and your pet)

_____

_____

_____

_____

_____

Index